Hurricane!

By Margie Sigman
Illustrated by Dan Grant

Scott Foresman
is an imprint of

Glenview, Illinois • Boston, Massachusetts • Chandler, Arizona •
Upper Saddle River, New Jersey

Illustrations

Daniel L. Grant.

Photographs

Every effort has been made to secure permission and provide appropriate credit for photographic material. The publisher deeply regrets any omission and pledges to correct errors called to its attention in subsequent editions.

Unless otherwise acknowledged, all photographs are the property of Pearson Education, Inc.

20 Chris Hondros/Getty Images.

ISBN 13: 978-0-328-50860-0
ISBN 10:　　0-328-50860-8

5 6 7 8 9 10 V010 13 12

Thursday Afternoon

"… Hurricane Drew is expected to become a Category 3 storm. Scientists at the National Hurricane Center predict it will hit the coast of Florida later this week." The reporter sounded grim.

Sam turned to his dad. "Will we need to evacuate?"

"No, I don't think so, Sam. We live inland, far from the coast. It's usually people who live near the coast who must leave their homes."

"It will be noisy, wet, and terrifying, but I think you'll find out for yourself in a few days!"

"What do you think of that, Reggie?" Sam asked his dog. "We move here from Indiana, and we get a hurricane! This is exciting!"

The two of them went outside. A slight breeze was beginning to blow, but overall, the weather was still good.

Early Saturday Morning

Sam lay in bed, listening to a sound that he'd never heard before. It was the wind making a low, steady moaning interrupted by sudden gusts. A tree branch flew by his window. *Is this what it's like at the beginning of a hurricane?* Sam wondered. Back home in Indiana they never had hurricanes.

Sam heard Reggie whining and whimpering outside his bedroom door. "Do you need to go out, boy?" asked Sam.

Still half asleep, Sam took the dog downstairs, opened the door, and watched as Reggie raced out. Then he went to wake his parents. "Mom! Dad! The wind's getting stronger!"

"Well, Sam, your first hurricane is on its way," said Dad. "I think we're ready. We've got supplies—water, a radio, flashlights, extra batteries, and plenty of candles. We'll need them if we lose power. Sometimes the electricity can be out for a couple of days until the power crews can repair the power lines."

Mom said, "Whatever you do, Sam, don't let Reggie out unless he's on a leash. Animals can get very frightened and confused in big storms. Remember when he ran away in that thunderstorm in Indiana?"

Sam had a terrible sinking feeling in his stomach. Should he tell his parents that Reggie was already out?

"Sure, Mom, okay," said Sam guiltily. "I better go get dressed."

Sam ran into his room and threw on some clothes. He knew how much Reggie hated storms, and there was no time to waste.

Downstairs, Sam grabbed Reggie's new red leash. *Maybe Reggie will be right outside*, he thought as he opened the front door.

Sam was surprised by how windy it had become. The yard was littered with small branches as well as leaves from the palm trees. A little child's blue ball rolled across the yard and into the street.

"Reggie! Reggie! Where are you, boy?"

Sam continued to shout his dog's name, but the sound of the wind drowned him out. Then it started raining. Conditions were changing from bad to worse.

Dad came to the door. "Sam, where's Reggie?" he asked, looking at the leash.

Sam couldn't meet his father's eyes. "Uh … I, uh … well, I don't know exactly." Then Sam blurted out the whole story to his dad. "Maybe if the wind dies down a little, I can go find him," Sam suggested hopefully.

"No, that's way too dangerous. We're going to need to stay inside because the wind is just going to get stronger. Don't worry, though. I bet Reggie is close by, and he'll be home soon."

Sam no longer felt excited about his first hurricane. All he cared about now was his dog getting home safely.

"Come inside, son. Let's see if we can find out exactly when the hurricane is going to get here."

Saturday Noon

Sam's mom had the weather channel on. "...**WARNING: Funnel Clouds Have Been Reported Along Coast. A Tornado Watch Is In Effect** . . ." said the ticker tape across the bottom of the TV screen. Just then, the screen went black, and the lights went out. Outside the window, palm trees were whipping around in a rushing, swirling wind.

"Time for candles and flashlights!" said Dad, trying to be cheerful.

"Mom, what are we going to do about Reggie?" Sam asked miserably. "I feel so bad. I was the one who let him out. I should've known better."

Mom tried to comfort him. "Don't blame yourself, Sam. We were so busy thinking about the hurricane that we forgot to prepare *you* for it! Animals can be a lot smarter than humans at times like this. Reggie will find shelter somewhere."

Saturday Afternoon

All Sam could hear was the nonstop roar of the wind and rain and a nagging voice in his head. *Where's Reggie? Why did I let him out?* the voice said over and over.

"Can't we take the car and look for him?" Sam suggested.

"I wish we could, Sam, but it's just too dangerous out there with all the trees. A falling tree can bring down a live power line or even crush a car! Besides, the wind is so noisy that I don't think Reggie would hear us calling him."

"Wait a minute," said Mom. "Did he have his collar on?"

"I think so, but I'm not sure," replied Sam, not understanding.

"If people find him they'll have our name and phone number. They can call us!" Dad said excitedly.

"But the electricity's out!" wailed Sam.

"It's okay, Sam. We're lucky. Telephones like ours still work in a storm!"

Sam looked at his parents' smiling faces. For the first time, he felt a glimmer of hope.

Saturday Evening

Hours later, Reggie still hadn't come home. By now, the front lawn had started to look like a shallow swimming pool. Tree limbs and debris were everywhere. One of the oak trees had fallen over onto the walk. What a mess! The phone didn't ring, not even once.

At last, the rain began to slack off a little. The electricity was still out, but on the radio they heard that the storm had moved on.

"How about having something to eat? What about a piece of fruit, Sam?" asked Dad.

"I'm not hungry," said Sam, too worried to eat. It had been almost twelve hours since he'd let Reggie out.

Finally, around six o'clock, the phone rang. Sam raced to pick it up.

"Hello?" said a man's voice. "This is Mack Daniels on Kent Street. Are you missing a dog?"

Sam couldn't believe his ears. "Oh, yes, sir, we are!" cried Sam, nearly stumbling over the words in his excitement. "Is my dog okay?"

"He's one lucky dog. He was hiding in a ditch under the road when the water started rising. He had to swim for it! Thank goodness, I just happened to see him and was able to grab him."

"Thank you very, very much, Mr. Daniels," said Sam with a catch in his voice. He handed the phone to his father who took down Mr. Daniels's address before finally hanging up.

"So, we'll check the weather report," said Dad, his eyes sparkling. "As soon as it's safe, Sam, you and I will go get Reggie and bring him home!"

Hurricane Safety

Hurricanes are dangerous storms. Everyone must be prepared. Before a hurricane hits:

- Get extra batteries, flashlights, and water. Be sure you have a radio that runs on batteries.
- Have an emergency plan for everyone in the family, including pets.
- Get food that doesn't need to be heated or cooled. You might not have electricity.

During a hurricane, always:
- Stay inside.
- Stay away from windows.

After a hurricane:
- Do not go outside without an adult.
- Do not play in ditches or puddles, or near fallen trees.
- Stay far away from power lines.
- Do not drink water from a faucet without asking an adult first.